A divine appointment is the Spirit-guided intersection of people's lives for God's purposes.

INTRODUCTION

The phrase "divine appointment" does not appear in the Bible. However, the concept is clearly immersed throughout scripture. In fact, the greatest divine appointment of all time was the prophetically predicted arrival of Jesus as a baby in Bethlehem. "But when the fullness of the time had come, God sent forth His Son, born of a woman . . ." (Galatians 4:4). This divine appointment with destiny was life-changing: "In His name the nations will put their hope" (Matthew 12:21). "Divine" implies supernatural engagement. "Appointment" implies intentional timing. Both of these circumstances were evidenced in the birth, life, death, burial, resurrection, and ascension of Jesus Christ.

Probably the two most easily recognizable divine appointments in scripture are the story of the woman at the well and the story of the Ethiopian eunuch. Both of these occurrences highlight supernatural engagement and intentional timing. The result was life-changing for both individuals involved. These stories are featured as part of this journal.

Where was the phrase "divine appointment" coined? It was likely popularized by author Oswald Chambers (1874-1917). He is most well-known for the devotional book My Utmost for His Highest, which has become a classic in Christian literature. In this book, we find tremendous spiritual depth, including this powerful statement: "God is the Great Engineer, creating circumstances to bring about moments in our lives of divine importance, leading us to divine appointments."

For the purposes of this book, we will use the following definition:

> *A divine appointment is the Spirit-guided intersection of people's lives for God's purposes.*

The thirty-day divine appointment challenge originated with a Church Growth class that I taught at the Seventh-day Adventist Theological Seminary at Andrews University. Most classes that I took while attending seminary required a lot of reading and book reports. I wanted to provide my students with something a bit out of the ordinary. The assignment was simple: pray every morning for thirty days for a divine appointment, and then journal the results. Almost immediately I received feedback by phone, text, and in person from excited students: "You won't believe what just happened . . ." At the end of the required thirty days, well over eighty percent of the students indicated that they intended to continue praying for divine appointments every morning for the rest of their lives.

One of the goals identified by the General Conference of Seventh-day Adventists is "Total Member Involvement," or TMI. The Life-Changing Divine Appointments journal provides a framework for every member to engage in ministry (TMI) based on appointments that God sets. Perhaps this journal becomes part of preparation work for a reaping evangelistic series. In the Oregon Conference, we intend to invite our churches to use this resource for all of their members during the last full month prior to launching a reaping series. Another option is to use this resource as part of a sermon series on divine appointments. You may want to consider going through the journal with your small group, church board, elders, or even for family worship.

Many of the stories shared in this journal are of a personal nature. God has been leading me on a journey of being more attentive to His providential leading. There have been so many missed opportunities in my life due to lack of attentiveness, lack of courage, or even lack of concern. I need the same challenge that Jesus gave His disciples in John 4:35, "Behold I say to you, lift up your eyes and look at the fields, for they are already white for harvest." As you embark on this thirty-day adventure with God, I pray that your experiences will motivate you to continue praying for divine appointments for the rest of your life.

BEGIN YOUR JOURNEY

This journal is intended to be used for thirty consecutive days. Each day there is a devotional, a coaching question, a real-life divine appointment story and space to journal any divine appointments that took place that day. At the start of each day, after you have read the material, pray that God will give you a divine appointment. Go throughout your day with anticipation, looking for God's opening providences. There may be days, where nothing out of the ordinary happens. On the other hand, there may be days where multiple divine appointment occur. At the end of each day, go back to your journal and record what took place.

As an encouragement for this journey, I am including a divine appointment experienced by one of my former students who was part of the thirty-day challenge in my Church Growth class. While it is doubtful that you will go skydiving for your divine appointments, there is no doubt that adventures lie ahead.

REAL-LIFE DIVINE APPOINTMENT
By Karina Sheldon

Photo: Karina Sheldon

Skydiving had been a bucket list adventure for most of my life. I had always put it off for one reason or another. Finally, when I was thirty-seven years old, I decided to literally take the jump and do it. Little did I know that even in this bucket list adventure God had planned a radical divine appointment!

On the day of the jump, I convinced my dad to jump with me. He agreed, and we headed out to the skydiving center. My dad asked why we had to drive two hours away from home to go skydiving since there were other places closer to home. I told him that this place had been recommended by a friend and it happened to be the only one on Groupon with a discount. We finally arrived, prayed together, and did our training in preparation for the jump. Then, as we headed over to meet our jump instructors, I heard someone call my name. I looked up to see a face that I had not seen in nearly twenty years. It was Korey, an old classmate of mine from high school, and now he was my tandem jump instructor. My dad and I were shocked.

The conversation we had with Korey can only be described as a divine-appointment conversation. Korey told me that he had been struggling lately and had asked God for a sign to show what direction he should go in his life. When he heard my testimony and how I got into ministry, he said that he knew without a shadow of a doubt that God had sent me there that day to help him.

In that moment, my dad and I realized two things: I was exactly where I was supposed to be, and the two-hour drive to this particular skydiving center, which was randomly recommended by a friend and also happened to be on discount (God knows I love a discount), wasn't by chance. My dad excitedly said, "God used your desire to skydive and created a divine appointment to witness! Wow! I would say He's jumping with us today for sure!"

I couldn't deny it! God had a plan the whole time! God used even this crazy skydiving adventure as an avenue to create a divine appointment where I could be a witness.

"For it is out of the abundance of the heart that the mouth speaks" (Luke 6:45 NRSV).

A synonym for the word "abundance" in this passage is "overflow." We simply cannot help but talk about what makes us passionate. In marketing, this is referred to as "word of mouth" advertising.

I remember experiencing this phenomenon while growing up in Walla Walla, Washington. My parents would occasionally take my sister and me to an off-the-beaten-path burger shop named Ice-Burg. They had become locally famous for their tasty food, especially their forty varieties of milkshakes. Fresh huckleberry (a wild mountain blueberry) was a seasonal favorite. I particularly enjoyed mixing flavors. Hot fudge added to anything usually ended up tasting pretty good. Every time we went, there was a long line for the drive-thru and the walk-up window. How were all these customers drawn to Ice-Burg? Simply by "word of mouth." I don't recall ever seeing Ice-Burg advertisements. Despite the presence of many cheaper and quicker options in the area, their business has thrived since the 1950s.

Jesus' disciples experienced an overflow in their passion. When asked to be silent about their faith, their response was this: "As for us, we cannot help speaking about what we have seen and heard" (Acts 4:20 NIV).

As you begin this thirty-day journey of praying for divine appointments, reflect on your own spiritual cup. How full is it at the moment? Are you ready for it to overflow? Commit to take time for Jesus every day through reading His word and prayer. As you do, your cup will begin to fill. The overflow is the sharing that will naturally result.

COACHING QUESTION

What will it take for you to have an "overflow" experience with Jesus?

_____

_____

_____

_____

There are very specific reasons to go to the grocery store. Either you are hungry or you plan to get hungry and need to stock up your pantry. Faye Mullins has a different purpose in mind. She believes that God has divine appointments prepared for her. She goes to the grocery store to meet people. Prayerfully, she asks God to lead her to the right person. Her experience with Jesus is overflowing, and she looks for opportunities to reflect Him to others. As she sparks new friendships, she does what comes most naturally to her. She invites them to her home for a meal followed by a Bible study.

If you have the chance to have a conversation with Faye, you will notice that she stutters. That has not slowed her down. Like the early disciples, no one can stop her from sharing her passion for Jesus. God has given Faye tremendous results. More than two hundred and fifty people have been baptized, and a church has been planted. All of this is happening in a secular part of the first world where it is considered difficult to reach people (Calgary, Alberta, Canada). Specifically ask God that you will to help you notice opportunities for divine appointments in the routine errands that you do today.

Pray at the beginning of the day that God will give you a divine appointment;
then journal the results here at the end of the day.

met a neighbor who is a Christian,
strongly believing in Holy Spirit.
been kicked out from a church - could be pentacost
very emotional, expressed it in our first conversation
told that he almost die, stated food health is
important. Watching TIW, but said the program
intent has changed. Don't know what he mean,
never revealed why program changed.

On winter day storm Jan 17 got up 7.30am
to shuffle shovel the snow. then used
snowblower, helping neighbors to clear the snow

Having someone who believes in you is a game changer. Israel was being dominated by the Midianites. Raiding bands would descend "like locusts" (Judges 6:5 ESV) upon their territory and consume their crops. Israel was left decimated and became "greatly impoverished" (Judges 6:6). We are introduced to Gideon as he is hiding for his life and threshing wheat in a winepress. This is not the picture of a bold warrior. Yet, an angel addresses him, "The Lord is with you, you mighty man of valor!" (Judges 6:12). The word "valor" comes from the Hebrew word "he·hā·yil," which denotes "heroes of strength," and it often refers to an entire army. Further affirmation of Gideon follows:

"Have I not sent you?" (Judges 6:14).

Gideon doesn't feel up to the task: "O my Lord, how can I save Israel? Indeed my clan is the weakest in Manasseh, and I am the least in my father's house" (Judges 6:15).
Now, Gideon hears the words that change everything:

"Surely I will be with you, and you shall defeat the Midianites as one man" (Judges 6:16).

"The Lord does not always choose for His work men of the greatest talents, but He selects those whom He can best use. Before honor is humility. The Lord can use most effectually those who are most sensible of their own unworthiness and inefficiency. He will teach them to exercise courage and faith. He will make them strong by uniting their weakness to His might, wise by connecting their ignorance to his wisdom."[1]

One of the most significant principles to remember when it comes to divine appointments is that God sets them up. God orchestrates an appointment between you and another person. This means that He trusts you. Just as God spoke words of encouragement to Gideon, He is strengthening you for mission today:

> *"Have I not sent you? . . . Surely I will be with you"*
> *(Judges 6:14, 16).*

COACHING QUESTION

How does knowing that God sets up divine appointments instill confidence in you?

_____

_____

_____

_____

---

[1] *Ellen Gould White, SDA Bible Commentary, vol. 2 (Washington, D.C.: Review and Herald Publishing Association, 1965), 1003.3.*

"Today is going to be a big day," I thought as I walked toward the car. It was the day I would be practicing the first sermon that I had ever written, with the help of my mentor, Pastor John T. Boston. In just two days, I would be preaching this sermon at a large church. I was twelve years old, and both excited and nervous at the same time. I had called my sermon "What Does Your Angel See?" I compared Ezekiel 10 with modern surveying technology, such as drones, and what our angels see and record about each of us, and I had a surprise ending planned.

Together with my family, the Boston family, and a local school chaplain, I chose a special spot to practice my sermon. We met at a popular rain forest national park, with waterfalls and spectacular lookouts. Most of the picnic spots were already taken. The only free table was in an undercover BBQ area, joined to another table where a family had set up for lunch. We asked if we could take the table adjoining theirs, and then we soon had lunch ready, and started to eat. The nearby family ate quietly and spoke softly as we talked, laughed, and interacted with the giant goanna (an Australian reptile), who had come over to inspect our lunch.

As we talked with the family, we soon learned that they had come to the park for a day visit, and that they were working temporarily on a project in the area. The family had recently moved to Australia from the Middle East, and they were Muslim. We spoke with them while we ate, and soon it was time to practice my sermon. I told them that I was going to be preaching, and that I had come to practice. Continued tomorrow . . .

15

PRAYER & JOURNAL CHALLENGE

Pray at the beginning of the day that God will give you a divine appointment; then journal the results here at the end of the day.

_____

_____

_____

_____

_____

_____

_____

_____

_____

_____

_____

_____

_____

_____

_____

_____

_____

_____

Photo: Tom, Hayden and Ryan

The inhibition to share our faith is something we seem to develop with age. I was in the middle of preaching a sermon in Nambucca Heads, Australia when a hand shot up to ask a question. A preteen boy had been listening intently, and to him it seemed to be the most natural thing to spontaneously respond to what he was hearing. I recognized his hand and answered his thoughtful question. After the sermon, I wanted to personally meet him and his parents. A couple of months later, I was preaching at a church in a nearby community. Hayden and his family traveled to hear me again. This time, I introduced Hayden to a pastor who helped him prepare his first sermon. Hayden shares the story in the "Real-Life Divine Appointment" section for yesterday and today. Hayden is bold about his faith and courageous in sharing. Recently, he preached his first evangelistic series in the Philippines, at the age of fourteen.

The parable of the good Samaritan is one of the most popular stories told by Jesus. It highlights the need for courageous engagement. The wounded man by the side of the road is clearly seen by both the Priest and the Levite, but they "passed by on the other side" (Luke 10:31,32). We can surmise their excuses: the wounded man was of a different nationality; they were running late; they didn't have medical expertise; they were afraid of robbers themselves. The third passerby had a different response: "he had compassion" (Luke 10:33). The Samaritan traveler rendered aid and sacrificed of his time and money to care for the stranger. Every time we engage, it will require something of us. The first step is the courage to do it.

Photo: Hayden at his baptism

COACHING QUESTION

What inhibitions do you need to let go of?

_____

_____

_____

_____

Photo: Hayden and Pastor Daron

I used a laptop to share my power point, and our small group gathered together. Under the table, I had a drone that was powered and ready to fly at the right moment. I started my sermon with a prayer, and I could feel the presence of the Holy Spirit as I started to speak. Everyone listened quietly while I spoke. I noticed that the nearby Muslim family had stopped packing up their lunch, and moved in closer and closer to listen, too. By the time I closed my sermon, the family had joined our group around the table. I shared the message about how much we would consider changing in our lives if we knew that we were being watched and recorded at every moment by a drone. Then I flew my drone out from under the table, over our heads, and to the other side of our picnic area—lights flashing, camera blinking. I posed a challenge to everyone listening: God and the angels are watching our every move. There is a record in heaven of all that we do. If you had a drone watching your every move, what would you change? I encouraged everyone to dedicate their lives to God, and to ask for His power to help us change. As I closed with prayer, I saw that the Muslim family also bowed their heads. I prayed that God would lead each of us to know Him better, and to remember that He is always present in all that we do.

After I had finished preaching, we spoke with the family who had joined us. We shared our experiences of a God who loves us, and is working for us. The family's mother came and hugged me and told me that God was using me. As we said goodbye, we left as friends—joined by God. I preached my sermon two days later to a full church. It felt like I had already preached, because God turned my practice sermon into a real sermon for Him!

Pray at the beginning of the day that God will give you a divine appointment; then journal the results here at the end of the day.

Pray for Brian uncle Benny, Gaius, Vincent. Osber to find Jesus in their hearts, and souls.

It was the fiftieth anniversary of the church that I had grown up attending. I had been asked to be the speaker for this special occasion. Memories flooded my mind as I drove into the church parking lot and entered the church. An older lady approached me and said, "My sons used to attend Sabbath School with you. They don't go to church anymore." This same sentiment was expressed by other parents as well. During the sermon, I invited anyone who had a son or daughter, brother or sister, mother or father who had left church to come forward for prayer. The center aisle of the church flooded and the tears flowed. Where is the hope in the pain?

When Adam and Eve sinned, God didn't send one of the angels to locate Adam and Eve to escort them into His presence. He didn't boom His voice through the celestial paradise summoning them. God personally walked through the garden looking for them. This picture of God seeking us echoes throughout the corridors of scripture. Jesus announces His mission:

> *"For the Son of Man has come to seek and to save that which was lost"* (Luke 19:10).

The fantastic news is that we serve a God who is always seeking us, even when we aren't looking for Him, perhaps even running the opposite direction. God is always at work.

"The Spirit is constantly seeking to draw the attention of men to the great offering that was made on the cross of Calvary, to unfold to the world the love of God, and to open to the convicted soul the precious things of the Scriptures."[1]

COACHING QUESTION

Does your heart hurt for someone who is not currently seeking God? How will you join God in His seeking mission?

_____

_____

_____

_____

_____

[1]Ellen Gould White, *The Acts of the Apostles* (Mountain View, CA: Pacific Press Publishing Association, 1911), 52.

As a nurse, I was often scheduled for shifts that caused me to miss church. Over the years, my spiritual journey slowly slipped, and, almost imperceptibly, I lost my hold on Jesus. I never felt like I didn't believe in God, but my actions and lifestyle were definitely outside of the values and beliefs that I grew up with and had practiced early in life. I needed a wake-up call! Many years passed, a divorce in my late forties came about due to wrong choices. My family continued to pray for me.

One day at work when I was just past sixty years old, I noticed a page from the book Steps to Christ taped to my medical cart. It spoke to my heart! It told of God's great love for me personally. It had been placed there by a nurse friend and coworker. I started praying for victory and deliverance in my life. I started reading the Bible and other spiritual books. The comfort of God's presence came back into my life. I asked my son, a Seventh-day Adventist minister, to re-baptize me. It was definitely a special Sabbath. Four of my grandchildren were there to witness my new birth in Christ. Jesus means the world to me, and I want to share His love. I pray for divine appointments so that someone else's heart can be touched just as mine was.

PRAYER & JOURNAL CHALLENGE

Pray at the beginning of the day that God will give you a divine appointment; then journal the results here at the end of the day.

_____

_____

_____

_____

_____

_____

_____

_____

_____

_____

_____

_____

_____

_____

_____

_____

_____

_____

_____

There are two clear indicators of what we value: time and money. Our calendar and our bank account are a litmus test regarding our priorities. Today, we are focused on how we use time. Scripture challenges, "We can make our plans, but the Lord determines our steps" (Proverbs 16:9 NLT).

One of the great challenges we face when it comes to time is the tyranny of the urgent. There always seems to be more to do than hours in a day. We cram our day full, scarcely reflecting on the opportunity that we have to live life on mission for Jesus. Here are a few practical recommendations to help align your calendar with missional living:

1. Begin the day with God. Give Him permission to interrupt your schedule.
2. Touch base with God during the day. Be in tune with the Holy Spirit.
3. Allow for fifteen minutes between appointments.
4. Preschedule your day to eighty percent, rather than one hundred percent.
5. Take time to listen to others. Ask questions, and show interest.
6. Limit social media and constant phone usage.

Creating margin in our lives will provide gaps in which the Holy Spirit may orchestrate divine appointments.

How different would your day be if Jesus took over your calendar and set your priorities?

_____

_____

_____

_____

"It won't budge!" Pastor Vong said with exasperation.

"Rock it back and forth," Saisa replied.

The two Laotian mission leaders tried over and over, but the truck was stuck like a soggy log. They stepped out of the truck into the cool, shallow river. They pushed with all their might.

"It's stuck on a half-buried rock," Pastor Vong announced.

"Let's dig it out then!" Saisa was always a problem solver. They dug with their hands, but quickly discovered they needed a shovel. So, two worn-out men headed for the nearest village.

"Can we speak to the village chief?" they asked. He wasn't there, but the villagers led them to Phan, the second in command. He was happy to help. Villagers quickly dug up the rock, and the truck was free at last.

"It won't start!" Pastor Vong said, groaning. The engine was waterlogged. Night sounds from the jungle reminded them it was now too late and too dangerous to travel anyway.

"You can stay with me tonight," Phan offered. The two missionaries smiled in relief. Maybe God had a plan, despite the frustrations.

That night the mission leaders enjoyed some rice and savory toppings with Phan. "Where are you headed?" he asked.

"I am taking Mr. Saisa to a nearby village to meet a young lady. She is active in ministry and maybe they would be a good match." Saisa looked down at his rice bowl and blushed slightly. Phan wanted to know what kind of ministry they were doing. The leaders glanced briefly at each other. Should they disclose their religion? In communist Laos, discussing religion is a sensitive matter. How much should they say? Continued tomorrow . . .

PRAYER & JOURNAL CHALLENGE

Pray at the beginning of the day that God will give you a divine appointment; then journal the results here at the end of the day.

When circumstances cause an interruption in my schedule, my immediate reaction is frustration, followed by tension. Many delays naturally take place in the process of commuting to work or traveling between appointments. Traffic congestion during rush hour, construction, an accident, or a flat tire all can throw off the flow of the day. There are other types of delays that are self-inflicted: having to run back home to retrieve a forgotten item, picking up a missing ingredient for your recipe from the grocery store, searching for lost keys or a wallet.

The consequence of these interruptions is a changed course for the rest of the day. For example, if I arrive fifteen minutes later to work, my path is likely to intersect with a different set of people than if I had arrived when originally anticipated. Could it be possible that the interruptions in our day can be used by God to provide intersections of our lives with others? Is a divine appointment waiting on the other side of our delay?

Next time you are faced with a delay, begin reflecting on whether God has an intentional purpose that will result from the interruption. This perspective will certainly help reduce frustration and tension. In fact, in hindsight you might be praising God for the very thing that seemed to be an annoyance.

How will you react differently to disruptions in your schedule?

_____

_____

_____

_____

Photo: Mr. Phan and Tom

Pastor Vong took a deep breath and responded confidently, "We are Seventh-day Adventist Christians. Have you heard of them?" A smile slowly spread across Phan's face. He jumped up and dug to the bottom of a drawer. He pulled out an old paper. Pastor Vong took it and exclaimed, "It's a certificate from the Seventh-day Adventist church, saying you completed all the Bible studies from Voice of Prophecy!"

Phan nodded his head seriously. "Fifteen years ago, I completed all the studies by mail. I did not know any Seventh-day Adventists. For the last twelve years, I have been pastor for the Church of Christ here in my village."

The conversation did not stop after supper. It continued all night long. The Holy Spirit worked through Pastor Vong to remind Phan of the truth of the Sabbath and the nearness of Jesus' return. This study was just the beginning. Phan began visiting the capital city often to learn more. An Adventist church planter went to the village to give him Bible studies in his home.

Finally, Phan made his decision to be baptized as a Seventh-day Adventist. When Phan went back to his Kamu village, he led his members to worship on God's holy day, the Sabbath. Saisa returned to teach some more. Soon, fifteen community leaders and members were baptized. Another three hundred individuals continue to be very interested.

But what about that truck? It revved to life the next morning as if it had never had a bath in the river! The mechanics back home could not find anything wrong. Did the same angel that placed the miracle rock also keep the engine from starting? Someday in heaven Phan will want to know!

Photo: Pastor in Laos with new believers

PRAYER & JOURNAL CHALLENGE

Pray at the beginning of the day that God will give you a divine appointment; then journal the results here at the end of the day.

Hydrogen Peroxide is fun to watch in action. When sprayed on a wound, it bubbles. Did you know that hydrogen peroxide is ninety-seven percent purified water? Water doesn't bubble when placed on a wound. The active ingredient is what makes the difference. It is the source of power. The bubbling demonstrates hydrogen peroxide is doing its cleansing work.

The book of the Bible that records the movements of the early Christian church is Acts of the Apostles. This book should more accurately be titled, "Acts of the Holy Spirit." Without question, the power and action in the book of Acts is driven by the Holy Spirit. He is mentioned no less than fifty-seven times in twenty-eight chapters. Acts 1:8 reminds us where the source of power comes from: "But you will receive power when the Holy Spirit comes on you; and you will be my witnesses in Jerusalem, and in all Judea and Samaria, and to the ends of the earth" (NIV). The Greek word for "power" is "dunamis," from which we derive our English word "dynamite."

"Despite three years of personal night-and-day, seven-day-a-week training by Jesus, these men were not equipped for any ministry without the Holy Spirit.[1]"

If we want dynamite power in our lives, we must be filled with the Holy Spirit. The bubbling over in our lives will be a demonstration that the active ingredient is at work.

---

[1] *Neil Cole, Organic Church (San Francisco: Jossey-Bass, 2005), 52.*

COACHING QUESTION

How fully are you tapped into the power available through the Holy Spirit?

_____

_____

_____

_____

34

It was Thursday night practice for the praise team at the church. One of the guitars needed an adjustment that required a hex key. Rather than running to a local hardware store, Sergio thought this was a great opportunity to get to know one of the neighbors. The first lady Sergio approached had three small children and was struggled to take the groceries inside. She was yelling at her children and dropped a gallon of chocolate milk on the ground. Sergio felt sorry for her chaotic situation. The lady shouted out that Sergio might want to look for a guy by the name of Sean in the apartment building, as he was a musician. Continuing his quest for the simple tool, Sergio tried the entrance door to the apartment complex. It was unlocked. This door was never unlocked! As Sergio looked at the list of names on the apartment directory, he had a dilemma—only last names were listed. He only knew a first name. After taking the first flight of stairs, Sergio knocked on a door. In response to the knock, a voice shouted out from behind the closed door, "Who is it?" Sergio explained that he was from a church, and they needed a hex key for one of the guitars. As soon as the word "guitar" was mentioned, the door flung open.

"Hi, I'm Sean." Sean didn't have the hex key, but made an offer that took Sergio by surprise. "I can play guitar for you." Sean had been drinking and was in the process of rolling his own cigarettes. How should Sergio respond? How would Jesus respond? Instead of returning to the praise team practice with a

hex key, Sergio returned with a guitar player. The group immediately embraced Sean and included him as part of the praise team. After rehearsal, they spent a couple more hours with him. Later that night, Sean sent a text message to Sergio. "Hey Serge, tonight was nothing short of amazing. I felt wanted and loved for the first time in many, many years. Playing music was just a bonus." Two days later, Sean played with the praise team at church. He was overjoyed.

Sean ended up spending Thanksgiving and Christmas with Sergio and his family. The church embraced him and became his new family. A short while later, Sean was baptized and is now an active member of this church. The Holy Spirit guided Sergio's steps that day, and the results were life-changing.

PRAYER & JOURNAL CHALLENGE

Pray at the beginning of the day that God will give you a divine appointment; then journal the results here at the end of the day.

I tightened the laces on my brand-new pair of Nike Air running shoes. Although the event had been tagged as a fun run, I was in it to win it. My sixteen-year-old lanky frame was built to be fast. I placed my foot on the very edge of the starting line and leaned forward to get a quick start. As the starting gun sounded, I shot out at Mach 3 speed. An open-bed truck that was driving in front and taking videos of the runners had to hit the accelerator to stay ahead of me. As I rounded the first corner, I glanced back and noticed that I was well in the lead.

Then, something happened—I started to gasp for breath and my legs started to feel like Jell-O. How could I slow down without being embarrassed? My sprint turned into a jog. As experienced runners passed me, I slowed to a walk. That day, I finished as runner number one hundred forty-six, and I learned a very important lesson. The right pace is critical for a successful race. At the highest levels of long-distance running competitions, pacesetters (also called "rabbits") lead the first part of a race to help runners maintain an appropriate speed so that they can go the distance.

This interesting Bible verse highlights the importance of pace:

> *"Since we live by the Spirit, let us keep in step with the Spirit" (Galatians 5:25 NIV).*

Based on this verse, it seems that it is possible to run ahead or lag behind God's intentions for us. The phrase translated "keeping in step" implies walking in a row or in rank according to a particular pace. Who sets the pace? The Holy Spirit does. Success in the race of life requires constant contact with the pacesetter. "Your ears will hear a word behind you, 'This is the way, walk in it,' whenever you turn to the right or to the left" (Isaiah 30:21 NASB).

COACHING QUESTION

How will you be attentive to the voice of the Holy Spirit today?

_____

_____

_____

_____

REAL-LIFE DIVINE APPOINTMENT
By Sergio Quevedo

Photo: Story Tract

It was June of 1885. Eleven Seventh-day Adventist missionaries (including four children) disembarked in Sydney with a passion to share their faith in Australia. They brought with them the latest in printing technology in order to produce pamphlets outlining their biblical beliefs. The group traveled farther south to begin their mission in the city of Melbourne. It was the middle of a particularly harsh winter. The weather was bleak—rainy, windy, and cold—and the response to their efforts was even bleaker. No one seemed interested. Just as quickly as a pamphlet was handed to an individual, they would toss it on the soggy ground or in the trash. John Corliss was ready to give up. On a particularly discouraging day, John took his final pamphlet, folded it up, wedged it between pickets on a nearby fence, and headed home. A divine appointment was in the making.

A man by the name of William H. B. Miller, a printer, was avoiding mud puddles on his way home from work when, out of the corner of his eye, he noticed a folded-up paper stuck in the fence, flapping in the wind. He dislodged it and took it home. As he read through the pamphlet, his interest was piqued, especially in the topic of the seventh-day Sabbath. Eventually, he was able to track John down just as he was sitting down one evening for family dinner. John was surprised to see the man holding the very pamphlet he had left in the fence. What had once represented despair had turned to hope. William shared with John his interest in the Sabbath topic and gave him an invitation for a speaking engagement at his debating society. John enthusiastically accepted. As a direct result of that meeting, seventeen people accepted the Sabbath and were soon baptized as Seventh-day Adventists.

Pray at the beginning of the day that God will give you a divine appointment; then journal the results here at the end of the day.

_____

_____

_____

_____

_____

_____

_____

_____

_____

_____

_____

_____

_____

_____

_____

_____

_____

_____

_____

The story of Philip and the Ethiopian eunuch is one of the clearest examples of a divine appointment in the Bible. We first meet Philip when he is selected to be a deacon in the fledgling Christian church. Those selected to this role were identified as having a "good reputation" and being "full of the Holy Spirit" (Acts 6:3).

Acts 8:26 records how the remarkable encounter of Philip and the Ethiopian eunuch took place: "Now an angel of the Lord spoke to Philip, saying, 'Arise and go toward the south along the road which goes down from Jerusalem to Gaza.'" As Philip follows the instructions of the angel, he encounters a man from Ethiopia as he passes in his chariot searching the scriptures. Philip is instructed to overtake the chariot.

"The Ethiopian represented a large class who need to be taught by such missionaries as Philip—men who will hear the voice of God and go where He sends them. An angel guided Philip to the one who was seeking for light and who was ready to receive the gospel, and today angels will guide the footsteps of workers."[1]

As Philip catches up with the chariot, he asks a simple question of the eunuch,

"Do you understand what you are reading?" (Acts 8:30).

This opens the door to an amazing conversation about Jesus as revealed in scripture, which results in the eunuch being baptized. I call that a life-changing divine appointment!

42

COACHING QUESTION

Where will an angel guide your feet on mission today?

_____

_____

_____

_____

¹Ellen Gould White, _The Acts of the Apostles_ (Mountain View, CA: Pacific Press Publishing Association, 1911), 109.

REAL-LIFE DIVINE APPOINTMENT

By Laura Taylor

It was hot and dry in sunny California where I was spending my summer knocking on doors and sharing Christian literature. Our team of young people gathered together daily to pray, worship, and share testimonies from the prior day. My friend Cesar began to share his experience.

He had been working across the street from me, and, unbeknownst to me, he had been having a particularly challenging day. No one seemed interested in his books, and not a single book had gone out. Then something amazing happened that boosted his spirits and kept him going. Whenever he asked for water at the door when he was thirsty, he was always met with two water bottles and the phrase, "Here is one for you, and here is one for your friend." Over and over he was met with this response to his thirst. All of us were incredulous as we heard his story. We worked close by each other, but I had been down the street some distance from him and not visible. Our group realized that the people he was speaking with must have seen his angel! We were amazed and curious about what his angel looked like to those people.

A few days later, another one of my friends, Thomas, was by himself talking with a woman on her porch. As the lady went inside to grab her checkbook to purchase a cookbook, Thomas asked her for a drink of water. She came back with two water bottles and said, "Here is one for you, and here is one for your friend." Shocked at her words, as no one had been with him, Thomas asked what his friend looked like. She responded that he was very tall and had been right beside him, smiling and nodding his head. Our literature evangelism team was so encouraged to know that angels were working among us.

Pray at the beginning of the day that God will give you a divine appointment; then journal the results here at the end of the day.

_____

_____

_____

_____

_____

_____

_____

_____

_____

_____

_____

_____

_____

_____

_____

_____

_____

_____

_____

_____

There are a number of words that start with "un" that we might use when considering having a spiritual conversation with a secular person: uneasy, unnatural, uncomfortable, and unpleasant. As we explore biblical approaches to these conversations, my prayer is that the "un" is removed so that these conversations become easy, natural, comfortable, and pleasant.

A couple of factors made it particularly hard for me to learn how to engage in spiritual conversations with someone whose views were different than my own. I grew up as a fifth-generation Seventh-day Adventist on my mom's side. Gladstone Camp Meeting in Oregon had been a family tradition for decades. Additionally, I was raised in Walla Walla, Washington, which has a high concentration of Adventists due to the proximity to Walla Walla University. Although I was passionate about my faith, my skills at sharing it were lacking.

This was clearly accentuated on an international flight when I was nineteen years old. I was seated next to an older gentleman of a different faith persuasion. My immediate impulse was to identify which doctrine I would clearly explain to him during our eight-hour flight. As I started into a Bible study on the state of the dead, he pushed the button summoning an attendant. His request was simple, "Can you find me another seat, please?" Ouch!

The journey to learn how to better communicate my faith has led me to discover several approaches that are easy, natural, comfortable, and pleasant. One of those approaches is coaching. The real-life divine appointment encounter that follows also involves a conversation on a flight, but with a very different outcome.

COACHING QUESTION

How will you practice asking more questions?

_____

_____

_____

_____

The commuter flight from Detroit to Minneapolis would take about ninety minutes. As I took my seat, I met a friendly young adult by the name of Jay. Due to his outgoing personality, I soon learned a number of interesting things about his life.

Jay was twenty-seven years old, and he was beginning an accounting career. He was headed to Minneapolis for a guys' weekend. As the conversation progressed, I continued to learn about him. He had grown up in a broken home, and he currently had a drinking problem. He also found it strange that his current and previous girlfriends were both Christians.

What approach should I have taken with Jay? Was he ready for one of the twenty-eight fundamental beliefs? How about the health message or the Sabbath?

I felt impressed that I should ask Jay questions with the goal of helping him identify next steps in his life. I resisted the urge to voice my opinions in favor of seeing where the Holy Spirit would lead the conversation. Jay had opened the door for the first question I asked: "Why do you think that you keep finding Christian girls to date?" Jay identified that there was probably something missing in his life and that it might be that he was attracted to that part of their lives. I continued, "Where would you like to be in your life spiritually?"

Jay held up a finger on both hands to indicate distance, "This is where I'm at and this is where I would like to be." Continued tomorrow . . .

Pray at the beginning of the day that God will give you a divine appointment;
then journal the results here at the end of the day.

_____

_____

_____

_____

_____

_____

_____

_____

_____

_____

_____

_____

_____

_____

_____

_____

_____

_____

_____

Jesus' disciples were hungry as they headed into town to find an all-you-can-eat buffet. They had a clear agenda driven by their growling stomachs. Perhaps they enjoyed some falafels and hummus with a nice cup of freshly pressed grape juice. Meanwhile, Jesus sat down by Jacob's well and had a divine appointment with a Samaritan woman that proved to be life-changing for her.

The disciples returned feeling satisfied and ready for an afternoon siesta. They were annoyed to see Jesus engaged in conversation. Certainly, He must have been hungry as well. Jesus had a lesson for His disciples: "My food is to do the will of Him who sent Me, and to finish His work. Do you not say, 'There are still four months and then comes the harvest'? Behold, I say to you, lift up your eyes and look at the fields, for they are already white for harvest!" (John 4:34-35).

As Jesus engaged His disciples in conversation, the Samaritan woman returned to the village and invited the entire community to come and meet the man who had changed her life. The disciples had not managed to bring one person from the very same village to introduce to Jesus. Why? They had an agenda. They were hungry. They wanted something to eat. Jesus had a clear message for them: "Lift up your eyes and look . . . !" (John 4:35).

COACHING QUESTION

How will you be attentive to "lift up your eyes" today?

_____

_____

_____

_____

At this point, it was clear that Jay had a sincere interest in a relationship with Jesus. "What will it take to get from where you are at, to where you want to be?" I probed. At this point, Jay went silent. I could tell he was grappling with this question on a deep level.

Finally, he spoke, "I'm afraid it would take a crisis to happen for me to get serious with God." The depth of the conversation had gone to a new level. I gently queried, "How does that make you feel?"

With genuine angst, Jay responded, "It makes me feel scared." Our conversation continued for several more minutes. I almost always like to conclude coaching with two questions. The first question relates to accountability. The second question addresses urgency. First, "Who can help you reach your goal?" If I were simply giving advice, it would be most natural to direct Jay to his girlfriend for help. However, coaching helps an individual identify and own their solution.

I was surprised by Jay's response, "My mom can help me get closer to God. She has recently come back to Him and I'm sure she would be glad to help." Now, for the final question, "When would you like to start?" Jay didn't hesitate to answer, "As soon as I get back from this weekend, I'm going to connect with my mom and get started."

How did Jay feel about this conversation? Was he pushing the button for the attendant to rescue him? No, quite the opposite. Jay thanked me for helping him get closer to where he wanted to be in his life. He shook my hand while we were seated. As we stood to disembark the plane, he shook my hand again. As we parted ways in the airport terminal, he shook my hand once more. I walked away praising God for such an amazing divine appointment, thankful that my seat had ended up next to Jay for a period in time orchestrated by heaven.

Pray at the beginning of the day that God will give you a divine appointment; then journal the results here at the end of the day.

_____

_____

_____

_____

_____

_____

_____

_____

_____

_____

_____

_____

_____

_____

_____

_____

_____

_____

There is a scientific phenomenon known as inattentional blindness. This occurs when a person does not notice significant details unless they are specifically looking for them. An experiment known as *The Invisible Gorilla*[1] illustrates how blind we can be to something obvious happening right in front of us. Participants were asked to view a video of people, dressed in either white or black clothing, who were passing a basketball between them. They were to count the number of passes between the people wearing white, while ignoring the passes of those wearing black. Amazingly, most of the participants failed to notice a person in a gorilla suit walk slowly onto the set, stop in the middle and thump his chest and then exit. How could something so obvious be missed? We as human beings are prone to inattentional blindness, or selective attention.

The Apostle Paul understood the importance of being intentional in order to connect with people. His experience in Athens highlights this. Athens was a pluralistic society. Competing philosophies found a voice in the public square, perhaps similar to the "soap box" experience at Hyde Park in London. Paul was determined to be intentional in order to be effective. He describes his approach, "Men of Athens, I perceive that in all things you are very religious; for as I was passing through and considering the objects of your worship, I even found an altar with this inscription:

> '*TO THE UNKNOWN GOD.*' *Therefore, the One whom you worship without knowing, Him I proclaim to you*" (*Acts 16:22-24*).

---

[1] *Christopher Chabris and Daniel Simons, The Invisible Gorilla: How Our Intuitions Deceive Us (New York: Broadway Paperbacks, 2009).*

There are several insights we can draw from this experience. Notice that Paul was observant of all that was happening around him: "I perceive." Second, he was pondering and reflecting: "I was passing through and considering." Finally, he identified a connecting point: "I even found an altar." Paul was on high alert looking for opportunities to advance the gospel. As a result, many individuals in the city became believers.

Let's not succumb to inattentional blindness. As we go throughout the day, may we have a heightened awareness to opportunities in front of us.

COACHING QUESTION

How will you live today with heightened awareness?

_____

_____

_____

_____

I love a good deal. As I drove on Highway 1431 from Cedar Park, Texas, heading home, I noticed a placard by the road advertising haircuts for $4.99. A recently constructed hair salon was enticing new business through this rock bottom price. As I sat down in the chair and gave the usual instructions of "Number two and a half on the sides and half the length off the top," I was feeling proud of myself for taking advantage of such a great deal.

The lady cutting my hair seemed burdened, and she began to share her recent life journey with me. Her sister had recently moved in with her as she was going through a difficult divorce. Finances were tight and the emotions were difficult to navigate. They didn't know where to turn for help. Her pain was palpable.

When the haircut was done, I thanked her, paid my $4.99 and hit the road for the two-and-a-half-hour drive home. As I walked in the door, my wife immediately noticed the haircut. I began to share with her how this lady had poured her heart out to me.

My wife looked me straight in the eyes and asked a penetrating question, "Did you share Jesus with her?" I couldn't believe it. It hadn't even crossed my mind. I had even just come from a church plant that was planning evangelistic meetings. What a missed opportunity! The lesson of that day has lingered with me. I must live life with a heightened awareness to the appointments God has arranged for me.

Pray at the beginning of the day that God will give you a divine appointment; then journal the results here at the end of the day.

_____

_____

_____

_____

_____

_____

_____

_____

_____

_____

_____

_____

_____

_____

_____

_____

_____

_____

_____

_____

Colossae was a church primarily made up of Gentiles. In his book to the Colossians, Paul highlights how our relationship with Jesus impacts our interactions in the workplace. In this context, we find one of the most significant passages in all of scripture on how to relate to secular people:

> *"Be wise in the way you act toward outsiders; make the most of every opportunity. Let your conversation be always full of grace, seasoned with salt, so that you may know how to answer everyone" (Colossians 4:5-6 NIV).*

"Outsiders" refers to those who are encountered in the workplace, who are not part of the community of believers. Paul is concerned about how believers interact with secular people. He highlights this later: ". . . that you may walk properly toward those who are outside" (1 Thessalonians 4:12).

The following principles should inform our conversations:

1. Make the most of every opportunity.
2. Use wisdom/skill.
3. Demonstrate grace.
4. Add flavor (seasonings) to their lives. The experience should transform.
5. Customize your approach to each person.

The seasonings we add are wisdom and grace. The language implies that these spices enhance the flavor of what we share, making it pleasant and wholesome. But how do we know what approach to take? If we take a look at the previous two verses, Colossians 4:2-3, we notice a word that is repeated twice: "prayer." Our lives should to be propelled forward through prayer. As we are connected through prayer, the Holy Spirit will give us the wisdom and grace required to season people's lives with the transformational message of the gospel.

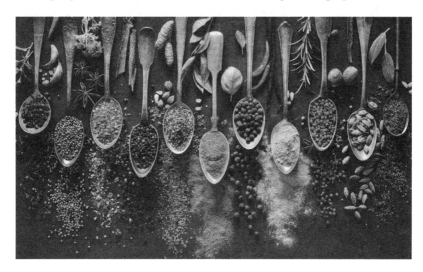

COACHING QUESTION

How will you add "seasonings" to someone's life today?

_____

_____

_____

_____

The Golden Corral certainly does not make my top ten list when it comes to favorite restaurants. I've discovered that all-you-can-eat is not necessarily a good thing at this point in my life. Self-control too easily goes out the window, and I'm left to live with the consequences. That being said, I've found that visitors from outside of the United States are intrigued by Golden Corral and want to give it a try. Such was the context of stopping at a Golden Corral with a group of friends from Australia.

As we were seated, the hostess took our soft drink order and gave us our first empty plate so that we could head over to the buffet. As we took multiple trips to engorge ourselves, she removed the used plates and refilled our drinks. As we neared a stage of lethargic inertness, I wondered what the tipping practice was for a place like Golden Corral? After all, we were making the effort to select our own food from the buffat (the correct word for an all-you-can-eat buffet). I decided to approach a different server to inquire. I was startled by the response, "We get paid $2.13 an hour."

When I returned to the table, I asked our server, Alicia, if it was true that she was only paid $2.13 an hour. She affirmed that this was the case and that five tables had not left a tip during her current shift. She added that she had five children and was unable to make ends meet. At this moment, we knew that God had arranged for us to meet this server, on this day, at this unlikely place. Continued tomorrow . . .

Pray at the beginning of the day that God will give you a divine appointment; then journal the results here at the end of the day.

_____

_____

_____

_____

_____

_____

_____

_____

_____

_____

_____

_____

_____

_____

_____

_____

_____

_____

_____

It is fascinating to study the history of the Moravian church. They were the first Protestant denomination to develop an urgency and plan for evangelizing the world. In the early 1700s, a man by the name of Count Zinzendorf organized what he called The Order of the Grain of Mustard Seed. Members of this group pledged three things:

1. Be kind to all men.
2. Be true to Christ.
3. Send the gospel to the world.

Sending the gospel to the world was accomplished through encountering whatever hardship necessary in order to preach the gospel. In their first missionary endeavor, the Moravians voluntarily became slaves so that they could preach the gospel to slaves. Others would enter leper colonies, knowing that they would eventually be overtaken by the disease and lose their own lives. They lived by the motto of the Apostle Paul, "I have become all things to all men so that by all possible means I might save some. I do all this for the sake of the gospel." (1 Corinthians 9:21-22 NIV).

The following quote has often been used to highlight a holistic approach to sharing our faith: "Christ's method alone will give true success in reaching the people. The Savior mingled with men as one who desired their good. He showed His sympathy for them, ministered to their needs, and won their confidence. Then He bade them, 'Follow Me.'"[1]

The first step in the process of evangelism is foundational. We must mingle. Simply put, we need to meet people where they are at.

---

[1] *Ellen Gould White, The Ministry of Healing (Mountain View, CA: Pacific Press Publishing Association, 1905), 73.*

COACHING QUESTION

Where do you mingle with others most frequently? How can this become an opportunity for divine appointments?

_____

_____

_____

_____

Wanting to be sensitive to Alicia's work schedule, we asked if she could spare a minute to sit down at the table with us. Believing that God had directed our path to Alicia, I asked her, "Do you believe in God?" She stated that she was a Christian, but because of all the trouble she was going through, she wondered if God really cared, or even if He existed. We shared with her that we were a group of pastors visiting from Australia, and that we believed that God had directed us specifically to her for the purpose of letting her know that He is real and that He does care. Tears began to flow.

After a short conversation, we asked Alicia if we could pray for her. Together we formed a circle in Golden Corral and lifted Alicia's case before our Father in heaven. Through her tears, Alicia expressed deep gratitude for us taking the time to visit with her. We assured her that it wasn't an accident that our paths had crossed. She gladly shared her contact information with us so that we could put her in touch with a church community who could surround her and her children with love.

Our team of pastors didn't want to simply provide words of encouragement, we felt compelled to demonstrate financially that God was looking out for Alicia. We pulled together a $92 tip. As our team reflected later, we identified this experience as the highlight of our trip. We had visited many amazing places, but the opportunity to know that God had set up an appointment in Golden Corral with one of his struggling daughters was priceless.

Pray at the beginning of the day that God will give you a divine appointment;
then journal the results here at the end of the day.

_____

_____

_____

_____

_____

_____

_____

_____

_____

_____

_____

_____

_____

_____

_____

_____

_____

_____

The word "but" is a showstopper. Perhaps you were dating someone when you heard this phrase, "You are a really nice person, but . . ." Whatever followed did not really matter. The fact was, that relationship was over. Jesus uses this word in Matthew 9:37, "The harvest is plentiful, but..." (ESV). The word "but" stands in the way of God's mission being accomplished. The rest of the verse reads, "But the laborers are few." Jesus is saying, "There aren't enough people who care about the lost like I do. I need human beings who will be my hands, my feet, my mouthpiece to a broken and dying world. Where are they?"

Many times, when Jesus comes to the church He only finds "Obediahs":
Oh, but I, ah . . . am too busy.
Oh, but I, ah . . . am too uncomfortable saying anything about my faith.
Oh, but I, ah . . . am already serving in other ways.
Oh, but I, ah . . . don't have the ability.
Oh, but I, ah . . . think someone else would be a better choice.

For every one of our "Obediahs," God has an answer. Notice how the passage concludes:

> *"Therefore pray the Lord of the harvest to send out laborers into His harvest" (Matthew 9:38).*

God can equip anyone who is willing to pray for His direction. It does not take a paid professional to do God's work. You should not wait around for church leadership to tap you on the shoulder and give you a green light to serve in some official capacity. Take initiative. God needs you, now! There aren't enough laborers! Remove the word "but" from your vocabulary when it comes to God's work.

COACHING QUESTION

What "but" needs to be taken out of your vocabulary to engage more fully in Jesus' mission?

_____

_____

_____

_____

Beulah lives in the isolated, wild west town of Lightning Ridge in the outback of Australia. Lighting Ridge is famous worldwide for opal mining. The wealth produced through this industry is not evident when driving around town. One creative feature in Lightning Ridge is the use of scrap car doors to write street names on. In the summer, the heat is so intense that mining machinery cannot operate. In this setting, Beulah serves as volunteer pastor of a small congregation.

One of the outreach ministries Beulah and her members are involved with is sharing literature at a stall in the local market. One day, Beulah was approached by a woman who said, "When are you going to come and share with my town, Weilmoringle?" Although Beulah didn't know where Weilmoringle was located, she assured the lady that she would be happy to visit her town. Despite her best intentions, Beulah forgot about her promise for two years. One morning she woke up before sunrise with a strong conviction, "Go to Weilmoringle, now!" Immediately acting on the promptings of the Holy Spirit, she called a friend and said, "We need to go to Weilmoringle, now!" As they drove through the red dirt desert, making one turn after another on abandoned roads, they finally saw a sign that welcomed them to the little town of Weilmoringle. Not only did they see a sign, but also a familiar face. As Beulah stopped her vehicle and got out, the very woman from the market greeted her and said, "I wondered when you would come!" As a result of obeying the Spirit's promptings without a moment's hesitation, God opened the door for a vibrant children's ministry in this remote outback town.

PRAYER & JOURNAL CHALLENGE

Pray at the beginning of the day that God will give you a divine appointment; then journal the results here at the end of the day.

GLOW is an acronym for Giving Light to Our World. GLOW tracts are small, pocket-sized pamphlets on various biblical topics, such as Help for Loneliness; A Better Future; America's Top Killer; Ancient Scrolls Discovered in Forgotten Caves; and An Intelligent Faith. The GLOW website features forty-nine different titles. GLOW tracts can be handed out in person or left in prominent places where they are likely to be picked up and read, such as bus stops, toilet stalls, and seats at an airport. This makes sharing GLOW tracts easy for anyone.

Dan Serns has made sharing GLOW tracts part of his lifestyle. He carries a couple titles with him wherever he goes. He hands them out when taking his morning neighborhood walk, to a server at a restaurant—literally, any time and all the time. He simply shares these words, "Hi, here is something that will brighten your day." Dan believes that God designs divine appointments for these interactions. Many times, he has handed the right GLOW title to the right person at the right time. Often there are deep spiritual conversations as a result. Sometimes they are life-changing.

Take a few minutes today to look over the titles available online and order some GLOW tracts to share. Perhaps your church will decide to begin a GLOW tract ministry. The members of some churches hand out thousands of pamphlets per year. [1]

---

[1] Find more information about GLOW at their website, https://www.glowonline.org/.

COACHING QUESTION

Can you identify a time where having a GLOW tract available would have blessed a person you met? What opportunities to share GLOW tracts can you identify?

_____

_____

_____

_____

REAL-LIFE DIVINE APPOINTMENT
By Dan Serns

Photo: Dan and Lois Serns

I'm amazed at how Jesus uses GLOW tracts to open up conversations about life and eternal things. When my wife and I go walking each morning I hand GLOW tracts to people in our neighborhood. A couple of years ago we were staying for a few nights in a hotel in the Baltimore, Maryland area. In the morning during our walk, I was handing out GLOW tracts as usual. I saw a new, bright red pickup truck with a guy sitting in it. I walked over to the open window and said, "Hi, here's something that will brighten your day," and handed him two GLOW tracts. I noticed his hand was shaking as he took them.

The next morning, we were walking in the parking lot when I saw the guy in the red truck again. I did not have any new GLOW tracts, so I just waved as we walked by. He backed out of his parking space and drove up slowly beside us. He said, "Do you have a minute? Can I talk with you?"
"Of course. What's up?"

"You gave me those papers yesterday. I read the first one, and it was my story almost exactly. I grew up a follower of Jesus but lost my way about fifteen years ago when my wife left me for another man. I made some seriously poor choices along the way and found myself in a very, very dark place in my life. Night before last I had a dream that Jesus came back and I was not ready. I was still shaking from it in the morning when you walked up and handed me those papers. I opened the first one called Am I Good Enough, and it told about someone who had almost exactly my story. God sent you. I came out here this morning hoping I would run into you again."

"Do you realize how much Jesus loves you to put this whole thing together?" I asked him. We set up a spiritual growth plan for him to get back to being connected with Jesus, God's word, and godly people. Then we prayed together, and he let me take a selfie. This was another providential appointment that only God could have set up. Please pray for Greg that he will stay focused on Jesus and His pathways.[2]

---

[2] *If you'd like to read the tract, enter this link into your web browser: https://www.glowonline.org/glow_tracts/am-i-good-enough/.*

Pray at the beginning of the day that God will give you a divine appointment; then journal the results here at the end of the day.

_____

_____

_____

_____

_____

_____

_____

_____

_____

_____

_____

_____

_____

_____

_____

_____

_____

_____

_____

Many times, we have interactions with people we will never see again. This type of divine appointment we can refer to as being a drive-thru. Perhaps we engage in conversation with the person sitting next to us in the airplane, or we interact as we check-out at the grocery store. We might spend a few minutes conversing with a waiter at a restaurant or a staff member at a hotel. The likelihood of ever seeing these individuals again is minimal. These divine appointments can be significant, even life-changing. However, they are one-time brief encounters and our future role in the spiritual journey of these individuals is limited.

There is another type of divine appointment that we can refer to as a dine-in. These take more time and future interactions are likely. The result is a deepening relationship and multiple opportunities to influence the person's spiritual journey. Examples include: a neighbor, co-worker, someone with a shared hobby, a classmate, or a business owner.

Sometimes when we have a divine appointment, it isn't clear initially whether it is a drive-thru or dine-in experience. The following story illustrates a type of interaction that is typically a drive-thru, but in this case ended up being a dine-in.

COACHING QUESTION

How can you be more intentional about listening to the voice of the
Holy Spirit?

_____

_____

_____

_____

REAL-LIFE DIVINE APPOINTMENT
By Timothy Taylor

When I was seventeen years old, I attended a training program on how to give Bible studies. As a student in that program, I was assigned an outreach territory and an outreach partner. My outreach partner and I were supposed to knock on the doors only within our territory and invite people to receive Bible studies. One particular day, however, I felt impressed to do something unusual. After arriving at our territory and praying together, I immediately had a strong sense that I should leave our territory and instead knock on the apartment doors just outside our assigned area. As I did so, I met a young man named Darryl who was a Pentecostal youth pastor. As soon as I mentioned Bible studies, he opened his door wide and said, "I would love to do Bible studies with you!"

Over the following weeks, as we studied the Bible together consistently, Darryl and I became close friends. I eventually had the opportunity to invite him to attend a Bible prophecy seminar. The first night came and went, but Darryl did not attend. My classmates and I decided to pray daily that Darryl would be convicted to attend the series, even though he missed the first night. The second night came and went, as did the third and fourth, but Darryl never came.

Finally, on the fifth day of the seminar, I received a startling phone call. It was Darryl! He sounded frustrated and exhausted as he explained, "I haven't been able to sleep at all ever since these Bible prophecy meetings of yours started!" He continued, "I can't stop thinking about them and how I must go! Can you please give me a ride tonight so I can attend the seminar?" Of course I was happy to do that!

Darryl came with me that night to the seminar, and he didn't miss a single night after that. At the end of the entire seminar, Darryl made a decision to be baptized and join the Seventh-day Adventist movement. Exactly one year later he even ended up attending the same training program I had been attending when I had first knocked on his door. As he went out to knock on doors himself, I couldn't help but wonder how things may have been different had I chosen not to listen to the direction of the Holy Spirit that one day when I left my territory to knock on Darryl's door.

PRAYER & JOURNAL CHALLENGE

Pray at the beginning of the day that God will give you a divine appointment; then journal the results here at the end of the day.

As Christians, we can unintentionally believe that when it comes to a secular or unchurched person, we are the ones who have something to offer. Our relationship becomes a one-way transaction: we give, and the other person receives. Although our desire is magnanimous when sharing the blessings we have experienced in our lives, it can be perceived by the recipient as having an air of superiority. When we ask a secular or unchurched person for a favor, the relationship instantly changes. They have something to offer us.

Jesus understood the relational significance of asking for a favor. As He encountered the woman at Jacob's well in Samaria, He made a request,

"Give Me a drink" (John 4:7).

This is perhaps one of the most profound and counterintuitive approaches to witnessing. Ask a favor. This is especially effective when the favor aligns with a person's hobby or passion. The relationship changes immediately. You have seen value in them and what they offer, not simply in giving them what you have. As you apply this approach, you will find new doors that open and a receptivity you may have never experienced before.

Photo: I asked my neighbor, Jacky, for help with a garden. He showed up on his tractor! Story to follow.

COACHING QUESTION

When have you asked for a favor from a secular or unchurched person? What was their response? How will you incorporate this practice in future conversations?

_____

_____

_____

_____

We had just moved to a fifteen-acre farm in Texas, and we needed some help curbing the rodent population. A sign by the road around the corner from our house offering "free kittens" seemed to be the perfect solution. As we pulled into the gravel drive, I wondered if God had intentions for this connection beyond the free kittens being advertised. We were warmly greeted by a couple named Jacky and Cindy who were in their mid-fifties.

I was fascinated to learn that they were organic vegetable farmers who sold produce to Whole Foods as well as farmers' markets. This piqued my interest, as gardening was something I thoroughly enjoyed. I decided to ask Jacky for a favor, and said, "I grew up gardening in the Northwest. I'd love to know how to grow a great garden here in Texas. Would you be willing to help me?" Jacky instantly lit up. This simple question ignited a passion inside of him.

"You bet I would," he replied. With that, Jacky left the room and then reappeared a couple of minutes later, toting several large bags of seeds. "Do you like okra? How about cantaloupe? Watermelon? Zucchini?" As I responded in the affirmative, Jacky exuberantly poured seeds into Ziploc bags. Suddenly, he paused then said, "How big of a garden area do you have?" I shared with Jacky that we were just getting settled and that I hadn't prepared one yet. "Not a problem," he quipped. "I can head over with my tractor and till up as large of an area as you would like."

One day as I stopped by to visit Jacky and Cindy, I noticed the retention pond they used for irrigation was almost dry. As I approached Jacky and Cindy in the field, I noticed the concern on their faces. "Tom, if we don't get any rain, we are going to lose our crops."

At that moment, I made a bold suggestion, "Let's pray to the God of heaven to send rain." As we joined hands right there in the field, I sensed this was an opportunity for God to show Himself powerful on their behalf. Over the next few weeks, my travels took me to other parts of the state. During prayer request time, we would mention our farmer friends and their desperate need for rain. About a month later, I dropped in on Jacky and Cindy to see how things were going. The moment they saw me, their faces lit up and they said, "Tom, you can stop praying for rain now. We've had so much rain, and just at the right time that we have actually experienced a bumper crop!" We again joined hands in the field, praising the God of heaven for bringing rain and answering our prayers.

Pray at the beginning of the day that God will give you a divine appointment; then journal the results here at the end of the day.

_____

_____

_____

_____

_____

_____

_____

_____

_____

_____

_____

_____

_____

_____

_____

_____

_____

_____

Photo: Tom, Sue and puppies in England

If you enjoy a hobby, there is no doubt that you like to talk about it. In one of my seminars, I ask attendees to turn to the person next to them and share about a hobby that they enjoy. The energy in the room immediately increases. In fact, it is hard to continue with the presentation due to the enthusiastic conversations taking place. Hobbies add seasoning to our lives. They tap into passions and stretch us to excel.

Shared hobbies are one of the most effective ways to build relationships with others. Churched and unchurched people enjoy various activities, such as: hiking, stamp collecting, playing guitar, fishing, scrapbooking, pickle ball, and golf. Rather than simply enjoying our hobby with friends from church, why not expand our circle to include those outside our faith community? The bridge created through a hobby transcends barriers and creates natural connections.

Our family enjoys the hobby of raising show-quality English Cream Golden Retrievers. We have met many amazing people from all around the world, resulting in numerous divine appointments. We have welcomed people for a meal or even to stay in our home that we otherwise would have never met. The network of relationships created through this hobby is extensive. For example, we have developed friendships with the doctors and staff at the local veterinary clinic to which we take our dogs. We make connections with those who adopt our puppies. The doors that open as a result of a hobby are significant. God desires for our hobbies to become an avenue to share Him with others.

COACHING QUESTION

What hobby do you enjoy? What opportunities can you identify to expand your connections with this hobby?

_____

_____

_____

_____

Photo: The "mushroom" pastor in Thailand

Muak Lek, Thailand, which has a population in the surrounding region of about fifty-thousand, is the location of a church-planting project. It was in this community that I met the Mushroom Pastor. To be clear, we are talking about edible mushrooms that are served as food. As an intentional approach to reach Muak Lek, Pastor Ruang became a mushroom farmer. This bivocational approach to ministry has enabled Pastor Ruang to make connections in this largely Buddhist community that would have been virtually impossible otherwise.

On Friday afternoon in Muak Lek, a busy intersection is crowded with dozens of market booths. More than half of the market is dedicated to selling produce and meats of all varieties. This is where Pastor Ruang's mushroom booth is located. Not far from his booth, a vendor sells deep fried grasshoppers and cockroaches. Another offers live crickets. This is Pastor Ruang's ministry context. Four afternoons every week, the scene repeats itself.

Mushroom business has been good. Every market day, around $90 (USD) is made. However, the goal is not the money, but the opportunity to forge relationships with non-Christians. Is it working? As I joined the worshippers on Sabbath at the church plant location, just a couple hundred meters from the now desolate market, I wondered what impact mushroom farming has had in the community.

During our delicious Thai luncheon (where we enjoyed lots of mushrooms), I was able to connect further with a number of individuals. Pastor Ruang introduced me to a lady who is a vendor in the market. I shared with her that I had visited the market the day before, and I asked her if she liked eating grasshoppers. She smiled and nodded her head. Pastor Ruang had been building a friendship with her as he has sold his mushrooms nearby her booth. This was her third Sabbath to attend church. I would call this mushroom evangelism! Pastor Ruang shared that he had just conducted a baptism of four individuals. Several others were in the process of preparing for baptism. The Mushroom Pastor literally lit up as he shared story after story of lives transformed by the gospel. I'm sure we will meet many people in heaven who enjoy eating mushrooms.

Pray at the beginning of the day that God will give you a divine appointment; then journal the results here at the end of the day.

_____

_____

_____

_____

_____

_____

_____

_____

_____

_____

_____

_____

_____

_____

_____

_____

_____

_____

Showing interest in someone's culture is one of the quickest and most effective ways of connecting. This obviously isn't saying, "I like Taco Bell," to someone who speaks Spanish. There are a number of meaningful bridges that build relationships in the context of culture:

1. You have personally traveled to the country they are from, and you can converse about places you have visited. Short-term and long-term mission trips provide an excellent opportunity for this. College-aged students may want to explore Adventist Colleges Abroad for a year of study overseas. [1]

2. You can speak a few key phrases in their language.

3. You have a close friend that is from their country.

4. You know something about the history or current news of their country.

5. You enjoy a particular food or dish from their country.

6. Your family heritage has roots in their country.[2]

One of the connections that has been beneficial recently is with Russian-speaking individuals who visit a food pantry where our family occasionally volunteers. Many individuals coming to the pantry are from the country of Ukraine and have arrived in the United States as refugees. A simple

---

[1] Find more information at https://www.acastudyabroad.com/.

[2] Resources for researching ancestry can be found at sites such as https://www.ancenstry.com/ or https://www.23andme.com/.

[3] Find more information about Project 143 at http://www.p143.com/.

"dobre utra (Добре утра)," which means "good morning" in Russian, puts an immediate smile on their face. Our family hosted two Russian-speaking boys from an orphanage in Eastern Europe through Project 143 for eight weeks during summers and four weeks during Christmas for a couple of years.[3] In addition, I have visited Eastern Europe multiple times. These experiences further provide a bond and ability to connect.

Every day, we have opportunities to encounter cultural diversity in the major cities of the United States. The phrase "melting pot" was first used in the United States around 1788. The term endeavors to identify the process of immigrating nations merging to form a new identity in America. Today, the notion of a melting pot has been superseded by the concept of a cultural mosaic or salad bowl. In a melting pot, all ingredients become one, whereas in a salad, all ingredients retain their identity while adding to the overall flavor. The salad bowl of the United States presents many opportunities to connect with people of other cultures. The uniqueness of each culture can be valued and celebrated. It can also be a great opportunity for a divine appointment.

COACHING QUESTION

What natural cultural connections do you have based on your life experience? How can you expand your cultural exposure to build new bridges?

_____

_____

_____

_____

Growing up, our boys loved to build sand castles at the beach. Silver Beach on Lake Michigan is a great place for families to gather during the summer months. The water is cool and refreshing, without any salt or sharks. On this particular day, our boys began constructing a sand castle with the girl next to them. They were fully engrossed as their imaginations ran wild. My wife made a comment to the mother of the girl about how well the kids were playing together. As I had noticed a different language being spoken between the mom and the presumed grandmother, I jumped in with a question: "Where are you guys from?"

The first answer wasn't what I expected, "We are from Chicago."
I decided to probe a little further, and asked, "How about before that?"
"Oh, we are from Poland," she replied. That opened up a pleasant conversation about a close friend of mine from Poland and the delicious cabbage soup (Kapusta) that he served us. I learned that Chicago has the highest concentration of Polish residents of any city outside of Warsaw, Poland.

As the kids finished their sandcastle and we prepared to go, we exchanged phone numbers. Our children had played together so well that we decided it would be great to get together again. At the beginning of the next summer, we received a phone call from our new Polish friend, Monica. She was back in town and was looking forward to connecting. We invited Monica, her husband, and their daughter to join us for a meal in our home, which they gladly accepted. A simple conversation relating to culture, along with our boys playing so well with their daughter, had opened a door with complete strangers.

Pray at the beginning of the day that God will give you a divine appointment; then journal the results here at the end of the day.

_____

_____

_____

_____

_____

_____

_____

_____

_____

_____

_____

_____

_____

_____

_____

_____

_____

_____

_____

One of the barriers to divine appointments is the misconception that we need to have everything together in order to be a witness. Perhaps we have been through painful experiences in our lives and hesitate sharing, especially with someone we have just met. The irony is that God uses our brokenness as one of the most effective ways to connect with others. Our very pain can become a source of healing. Growing up on a small farm, one of my chores was to clean out the goat pens, haul the manure to the garden, and then till it into the soil. Our garden flourished. This life lesson taught me that the manure of life makes great fertilizer. Nothing is wasted with God. When we take a B, C, or even Z path in our lives, God can redeem the time. He will use our detours in life to help us relate to the brokenness in other people's lives.

How can we know when it is appropriate to be vulnerable? The third person in the conversation must be the Holy Spirit. We will feel a nudge, an impression, or a conviction that we must share. We may try to push it aside. But when we step over the edge and open our heart as a response to God's leading, we may be surprised at how He works. I've experienced a complete change of direction in a conversation once I've taken the risk to be vulnerable.

Unchurched and secular people are not looking for someone who has all the answers or who has it all together. They are looking for someone who is authentic. The Apostle Paul puts it this way: "But He said to me, 'My grace is sufficient for you, for my power is made perfect in weakness.' Therefore, I will boast all the more gladly about my weaknesses, so that Christ's power may rest on me" (2 Corinthians 12:9 NIV). If we want to experience powerful divine appointments, being real about our weaknesses and past pains is one of the most effective ways to see that happen.

How ready are you to pull the mask off? What is the potential blessing that
God can bring to others through your brokenness?

_____

_____

_____

_____

REAL-LIFE DIVINE APPOINTMENT

By Buster Swoopes Jr.

I enjoy teaching our fundamental beliefs in class at an Adventist university. We have a wonderful time as we discuss not only the theory of our beliefs, but also the practical aspects of them. One particular morning, after my personal devotional and prayer time, I really felt impressed by the Holy Spirit to add my abuse survival story to the Great Controversy lecture. I proverbially scratched my head as to how I was going to make that fit, but the sense and calling was too strong, and I yielded to the Spirit.

As I entered the classroom that morning a young lady who is not in my class came up to me as I opened the door and said, "God told me I need to be in your class today." Wow! I was startled, but I felt as though God was moving. I taught the class and went into my survival story. The class was somber, yet captivated in seeing how God wins in our lives even when times seem dark. After the class, the young lady came up to me and shared how she was also a survivor of abuse and never really got the help she needed. She then started crying, as she knew why God called her to come to my class that particular day. We were able to get her connected with a great Christian counselor who has been helping her make huge strides in her recovery. All because all involved were willing to listen to God's voice guiding us. Indeed, God wins even when times seem dark, as His light reflects off of us.

Pray at the beginning of the day that God will give you a divine appointment; then journal the results here at the end of the day.

_____

_____

_____

_____

_____

_____

_____

_____

_____

_____

_____

_____

_____

_____

_____

_____

_____

There was an unusual award given in every class at my elementary school at the end of the school year. Each class would nominate a "Courtesy Prince" and a "Courtesy Princess." The eighth-grade class selected a "Courtesy King" and "Courtesy Queen." Those selected for this award had consistently demonstrated kind behavior toward others. There was a girl in the class ahead of me that won every single year, including the finale when she was named "Courtesy Queen" of the eighth grade.

Why was her selection so predictable? Julie always made others feel better about themselves. She was an encourager. She was kind. Julie continued her courtesy into high school (where awards were no longer given) and into adulthood. To this day, Julie is one of the kindest and most thoughtful individuals you could meet. Jesus shines through her and it reflects on those around her. Fortunately, kindness isn't something that is inherited, rather it is a modeled behavior that can be learned. We can intentionally choose to be kind in our words and actions.

Roman Lubetzky's experience in the Dachau concentration camp inspired his son Daniel to name his nut bar business KIND. Roman was barely clinging onto life and hope when a kind-hearted German soldier threw a potato to him when no other soldiers were looking. He credits that kind act to his survival in the camp. Daniel created a business that promotes and celebrates kindness. He describes kindness as a "net happiness aggregator" because it makes the person you are helping feel better, but it also makes you feel better. [1]

Acts of kindness don't have to be elaborate. In fact, they are typically simple and spontaneous: giving up your seat, letting someone else go ahead of you, opening the door, smiling, or helping someone carry their groceries. Jesus equates these small acts as being monumental in heaven's eyes. "And whoever gives one of these little ones even a cup of cold water because he is a disciple, truly, I say to you, he will by no means lose his reward" (Matthew 10:42 ESV). Acts of kindness warm the heart of the person receiving them, and just might result in a divine appointment, too.

---

[1] Daniel Lubetzky, *Do the KIND Thing: Think Boundlessly, Work Purposefully, Live Passionately* (New York: Ballantine Books, 2015), 211.

COACHING QUESTION

On a scale of 1 to 10, how in tune are you to small acts of kindness toward others? What will it take to move your responsiveness up the scale?

_____

_____

_____

_____

REAL-LIFE DIVINE APPOINTMENT

By Logan Schultz

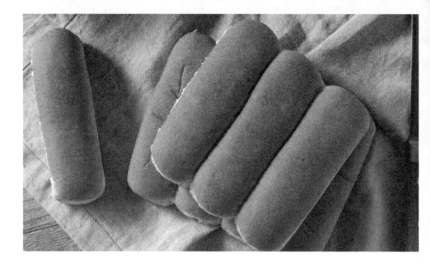

One day when my wife was serving lunch at our boys' school, there was an overage of hot dog buns. Rather than throw them out, my wife asked me to drop by a food bank and donate them. I had been presenting a two-day seminar for pastors, so I first reflected on my class and someone who might need them. God brought a person to my mind, and I had the packages of buns waiting at his table as he arrived the next morning.

Here is his account:
Thank you again for those hot dog buns. It meant more than you think. We love our churches, and it is awesome to see God in action. However, we have been really stressed about our housing situation, with no relief in sight. Sarah and I have been feeling especially discouraged the last few days.

I went to the Adventist Book Center yesterday and purchased a case of Big Frank hot dogs for the kids' lunches. I put them in the back of the car. I looked at them and, laughing to myself, thought of all the hot dog buns I would need. I get to the session this morning and find that you have left me great amounts of hot dog buns! Crazy! I just had to tell the Lord thank you! It helped me to realize that He isn't missing anything. If He cares that much to supply something as simple as hot dog buns, He certainly will supply our housing need. It may not seem like a big deal, but it sure cheered and encouraged our hearts. Thank you again, brother!

PRAYER & JOURNAL CHALLENGE

Pray at the beginning of the day that God will give you a divine appointment; then journal the results here at the end of the day.

I have made some pretty creative mistakes in my life. As a teenager, I was working on a dairy farm and lifted the tractor bucket loaded with manure too high, tipping the entire machine forward onto the manure spreader. It was a smelly mistake and my last day on the job. When I was nineteen, I missed a flight in Israel because I did not read the ticket in military time. I showed up twelve hours late for my flight. On that same trip, I accidently walked into a military zone. If it was not for a severe rain storm, I could have easily been shot. On my first Sabbath in a new church as the youth pastor, I went to turn on the gym lights and accidently set off the fire alarm. Most mistakes are relatively inconsequential. We learn from them and move on.

Sometimes the mistakes of others lead us down a path that can look pretty dark. As Joseph was sold as a slave in Egypt and later falsely accused and thrown into prison, he must have been thinking, This is a mistake! The injustice of what Joseph encountered was profound. Joseph's brothers set in motion a series of events that forever changed the course of his life. Years later as they stood before Joseph as second-in-command of Egypt, they were fearful for their lives. Joseph had God's perspective on his life journey:

> *"But as for you, you meant evil against me, but God meant it for good, in order to bring it about as it is this day, to save many people alive" (Genesis 50:20).*

Whether a mistake is seemingly inconsequential or profound, God's purpose prevails. Begin to look for God's providential leading next time you encounter a mistake. That mistake may turn out to be a miracle.

Catching a bus to the wrong hotel resulted in a divine appointment. Story to follow.

COACHING QUESTION

How does looking for divine appointments through mistakes challenge you?

_____

_____

_____

_____

REAL-LIFE DIVINE APPOINTMENT
By Kris Lenart

I had been invited to speak for a church planting conference in North Carolina. As a lay person, I have been very active in church planting in my home country of Austria. Arrangements had not been made for me to be picked up at the airport, so I called the hotel. When the van arrived to pick me up, they notified me that I was not staying at their hotel, but that my reservation was likely at their other nearby location.
The driver, named Tony, was happy to take me there.

Upon arrival, I walked up to the front desk and presented my identification. The response surprised me further: "Mr. Lenart, you are not booked here!" With that, the driver took me back to the first hotel. At this point, I realized that this was a very unusual situation and I said to the Lord, "What are you preparing? This looks like providential guiding!" We arrived back at the first hotel only to identify that there was a third hotel also in the area and that my reservation was at that one. My driver didn't hesitate. He was determined to help me arrive at my destination. At this point, I asked the driver,

"Where are you from?"
He responded, "Bulgaria."
"Which town?" I queried.
"Plovdiv," he replied.
"Do you know a person by the name of Malin who does woodwork?"
"Yes!" Tony responded, "But where do you know him from?"

I shared with Tony that I had been to Bulgaria probably eight different times holding seminars for the Seventh-day Adventist Church. Surprised, Tony shared with me that he was a Seventh-day Adventist church member in Bulgaria, but had stopped going to church when he arrived in the United States a number of years ago. I thanked Tony for his persistence in helping me get to the right hotel, then I invited him to attend the seminars the next day.

Tony arrived and was warmly welcomed by the church. When an appeal was made during the worship service, he was the first person to go forward in response. This divine appointment was such an adventure with God. Who would have thought that getting so many things wrong would put me exactly in the right place!

Pray at the beginning of the day that God will give you a divine appointment; then journal the results here at the end of the day.

_____

_____

_____

_____

_____

_____

_____

_____

_____

_____

_____

_____

_____

_____

_____

_____

_____

_____

_____

A Seventh-day Adventist study on nurture and retention discovered that for every one hundred new members that join the church, forty-two leave. If you attended an Adventist Academy, reflect back on your graduating class. How many are still active in the church? We can quickly concede that these statistics are correct and very disheartening.

The group that seems to be the most vulnerable for leaving the church is between the ages of eighteen to twenty-nine. A study among all religious groups in America conducted by the Public Religion Research Institute discovered the following: "Today, nearly four in ten (39%) young adults (ages 18-29) are religiously unaffiliated—three times the unaffiliated rate (13%) among seniors (ages 65 and older). While previous generations were also more likely to be religiously unaffiliated in their twenties, young adults today are nearly four times as likely as young adults a generation ago to identify as religiously unaffiliated."[1]

During young adulthood, many major decisions are made: Where should I go to college? What should I study? Who should I date or marry? Where do I want to live? The role of faith naturally goes through a transition from borrowed faith (the faith of my parents) to a personalized and mature faith. This shift is essential, but it is often bumpy and many times not successfully navigated. As a result, young adults leave the church they grew up in and chart a different course for their lives.

No doubt, you have previous friendships with individuals who have left the church. Renewed acquaintances can be one of the most impactful types of divine appointments. Begin praying for these individuals and watch to see what God will do.

---

[1] *Betsy Cooper, Daniel Cox, Rachel Lienesch, and Robert P. Jones, Ph.D., "Exodus: Why Americans are Leaving Religion—and Why They're Unlikely to Come Back," PRRI, (September 22, 2016): https://www.prri.org/research/prri-rns-poll-nones-atheist-leaving-religion/.*

COACHING QUESTION

What connection can you make this week with a previous classmate or family member that has left the church?

_____

_____

_____

_____

I had been preaching on the Texas-Mexico border. Part of my sermon emphasized the significance of divine appointments. As I began the seven-hour drive home, I came to the border check. There were three lanes from which to choose. Being pretty much on autopilot, I started to move my car to the left lane where the line seemed to be most promising for quick processing. As soon as I navigated my car into the left lane, I felt a strong conviction to change lanes. Although I thought this to be a bit odd, I immediately steered into the middle lane.

I looked up to see a man approaching me with a German Shepherd on a leash beside him. I have a natural aversion to German Shepherds as I was attacked by one as a young boy. The fear that I instinctively felt shifted to amazement. I recognized the officer who was leading the dog. His full name instantly shot into my mind. I extended my hand and greeted him, "James Wilson, Tom Evans. Great to see you." He was completely shocked and invited me to pull through as he wanted to take a short break so that we could visit.

As I spent a few minutes visiting with James, I discovered that he hadn't attended church since we graduated from high school together. He had a large family and was living in a border town. I prayed with him and we exchanged contact information. Later I followed up with an email letting him know how significant our interaction was. I believed that God had intentionally caused our paths to intersect that day because of a few reasons:

1. The border crossing was 2250 miles (a thirty-two-hour drive) from where we went to school together.
2. I would have completely missed him if I had stayed in the lane that I originally navigated toward.
3. I recognized him and remembered his full name even though we hadn't seen each other for twenty years.

God desires to see those who have walked away come back to Him. Your connection through a divine appointment could be the spark that reignites their spiritual journey.

PRAYER & JOURNAL CHALLENGE

Pray at the beginning of the day that God will give you a divine appointment; then journal the results here at the end of the day.

I was just starting full-time pastoral ministry when the first Valuegenesis study was conducted by the Seventh-day Adventist Church. The goal was to identify how the home, church, and school could work collaboratively together in the development of faith. I clearly remember a key finding regarding the influence of the home. The two most significant factors to mature faith development were family worship and opportunities to serve. This had a profound impact on me, both as a youth pastor and as a parent. Subsequent research continued to highlight these two areas.

> Valuegenesis discovered the seriousness of building quality family, worship that is meaningful and relevant because parents focus their worship on everyday practical lessons that relate to their children and they share the leadership among all family members. Learning to help at home and doing service activities as a family, not waiting for the church or Adventist school to provide the opportunity, along with setting limits on how much time is spent with video games and computer and television use will provide the best opportunity to build a mature faith.[1]

One of the challenges of the teenage years (and for many adults) is a struggle with self-worth. Scripture has thought-provoking counsel: "When you do things, do not let selfishness or pride be your guide. Instead, be humble and give more honor to others than to yourselves" (Philippians 2:3 NCV). Humility, rather than a focusing on building up oneself seems to be the tenor of scripture. As children of God, we are all innately of infinite value. Without trivializing the complexity of factors contributing to low self-worth, humility and service to others provide a perspective on life that is emotionally healthy. As we focus on serving others, there is a reciprocal boost to our own sense of well-being. Mayo Clinic identified that serving others decreases the risk of depression. [2]

---

[1] *V. Bailey Gillespie, "Studies suggest ways church can develop faith in its young people," Adventist News Network, (May 3, 2010): https://news.adventist.org/en/all-commentaries/ commentary/go/-/studies-suggest-ways-church-can-develop-faith-in-its-young-people/.*

[2] *"Helping People, Changing Lives: The 6 Health Benefits of Volunteering," Mayo Clinic, (May 18, 2017): https://www.mayoclinichealthsystem.org/hometown-health/speaking-of-health/ helping-people-changing-lives-the-6-health-benefits-of-volunteering/.*

COACHING QUESTION

What volunteer opportunities can you identify? What is the next step to become involved?

_____

_____

_____

_____

Photo: Andre, Tom and Lukas at PACS

As a family, we have had an opportunity to visit many countries. On most of the trips overseas, my family joins me for a speaking engagement followed by several extra days for vacation. Recently, I asked our boys to share with me which one of the trips was their favorite? Without hesitation, they said "Laos."

The irony of their response struck me. Laos is a third-world, communist country. We slept on hard beds and took cold showers, with just a trickle of water. We ate at a restaurant where we saw cooked bugs in the food. My youngest son was sick for more than a month afterward. This was their favorite trip? The visit to Laos was on a mission trip sponsored by ASAP Ministries (Advocates for Southeast Asians and the Persecuted). They were part of making a difference in the lives of others. This entire trip was full of divine appointments. Volunteering and serving others gave them a joy that surpassed their other exciting adventures around the globe.

Volunteering close to home is important as well. It heightens our awareness of the needs around us and provides multiple opportunities for divine appointments. We have committed to support the ministry of Portland Adventist Community Services by volunteering on a regular basis. In particular, we enjoy serving clients in the food store. Qualified shoppers receive points based on the size of their family and select food from various categories at no cost. Our job is to help guide them through the store as they make their selections.

One particular gentleman was not selecting anything that required cooking. As I conversed with him, I discovered that he was living in his car. I called my youngest son over to meet him. My son had never met anyone before who lived in their car. The man shared that he had applied for part-time work at the post office over the holiday season. I asked him if it would be ok to pray with him about that. We bowed our heads right there in the store and prayed together. Simple divine appointments like this happen consistently when we make volunteering a priority in our lives.

Pray at the beginning of the day that God will give you a divine appointment; then journal the results here at the end of the day.

_____

_____

_____

_____

_____

_____

_____

_____

_____

_____

_____

_____

_____

_____

_____

_____

_____

_____

Tall Poppy Syndrome is a cultural phenomenon that is present in some countries of the world. It is the tendency to fault-find, criticize, and tear down a person whom is perceived as having reached a level of success, achievement, or position.

Rather than having their successes celebrated, the person is pummeled with disparaging comments. This happens both directly and behind their backs with the intention of cutting down the "tall poppy" so that all are on the same level. The capitalistic culture of the United States naturally produces winners and losers. This competitive climate also impacts in a detrimental way the practice of affirming and building others up.

The solution to the above challenges is to create a culture of affirmation and gratitude. After healing ten lepers, Jesus clearly identified the significance of this practice: "One of them, when he saw he was healed, came back, praising God in a loud voice. He threw himself at Jesus' feet and thanked him—and he was a Samaritan. Jesus asked, 'Were not all ten cleansed? Where are the other nine? Has no one returned to give praise to God except this foreigner?' Then he said to him, 'Rise and go; your faith has made you well'" (Luke 17:15-19). Not only do these verses highlight the importance of expressing gratitude, but they also identify how rarely it takes place. In this case, the practice was followed by only 10 percent. Because it is so countercultural, the habit of affirming others will certainly produce some unexpected divine appointments.

The Five Love Languages concept has identified "words of affirmation" as being one of the love languages of a significant portion of the population.[1] I once coached a couple where the husband identified this as his love language. The wife struggled with affirmation, and stated, "I won't give a compliment unless he really has earned it." She eventually determined to make an effort to give one genuine compliment per day. The next time I met with this couple, his demeanor had transformed. It was like water on a parched plant. He had come alive! We can have this impact on others on a daily basis through cultivating a culture of affirmation.

---

1 Gary Chapman, The 5 Love Languages: The Secret to Love that Lasts (Chicago: Northfield Publishing, 2015).

COACHING QUESTION

On a scale of 1 to 10, how consistently do you affirm others? What would it take to move up the scale a couple of points?

_____

_____

_____

_____

Photo: Daniils and Andris at Costco

We had just left the Chicago airport after picking up the two boys we were hosting from an orphanage in Latvia. Our plan was to stop by a Costco on the way home so that we could purchase groceries for our expanded family. Visiting Costco is always an adventure with food sampling strategically positioned throughout the store.

As we finally arrived at the register to check out, the older boy (age eight) became fascinated with the remote scanning device. The highly intuitive cashier handed the device to him and let him finish scanning the groceries. The joy on his face was infectious. We thanked her for taking an interest, and asked for a photo with the boys. I also took note of her name. Before we left the store, I stopped by the customer service counter and picked up a feedback form. After we arrived at home, I located an email and sent a letter of appreciation, along with the photo. To my surprise, the photo and letter were published in the Costco newsletter.

As I reflect back on this encounter, I wonder why opportunities like this have so often escaped me. A couple minutes invested can be a source of encouragement to someone. I can't say for certain that this experience was a divine appointment. For an eight-year-old boy, who had just arrived from an orphanage, it certainly created a burst of joy. It also further established our appreciation of Costco. This quote highlights an interesting dynamic: "The enthusiasm of the guest experience can never rise any higher than the enthusiasm of your own employees."[2] This enthusiastic cashier added some joy to our day; the least we could do was affirm her effort.

---

[2] Joel Manby, *Love Works: Seven Timeless Principles for Effective Leaders* (Grand Rapids, MI: Zondervan, 2012), 60.

Pray at the beginning of the day that God will give you a divine appointment; then journal the results here at the end of the day.

_____

_____

_____

_____

_____

_____

_____

_____

_____

_____

_____

_____

_____

_____

_____

_____

_____

The dynamics of divine appointments are unique in that God is intentional in arranging them, but they are a surprise to us in most cases. I'm the type of person who likes to have my life charted out. It is the choleric side of my temperament coming out. This verse stretches and challenges me:

"Many are the plans in a person's heart, but it is the Lord's purpose that prevails" (Proverbs 19:21 NIV).

We should always submit our plans to God's veto power. We can press on with our own agenda; the value that God places on freedom of choice allows us to do that. However, we will soon realize that God being in the driver's seat will result in more purposeful living.

When it comes to divine appointments our responsibility is to mingle and to be available. Throughout this journal, different contexts and approaches have been identified. Following these principles can provide the most fertile soil for life-changing divine appointments to occur. However, when it comes to being led by God, we should expect some surprises. God sees what we don't. He is preparing people we wouldn't expect. He will take us where we would otherwise never go. He will open doors that seemed locked shut. Are you ready to sign up for the adveture?

COACHING QUESTION

How open are you to the surprise element of divine appointments? How will you balance planning and spontaneity?

_____

_____

_____

_____

It was my first time to visit Adelaide, Australia. I had been invited to present a seminar, "Spiritual Conversations with Secular People." As we gathered for tea (dinner) on Saturday evening, I looked across the fence and noticed that the church bordered a large city park. In the middle of the park, a group of individuals had gathered with their dogs. My eyes immediately focused on a cream golden retriever. Our family raised these dogs and I felt confident that a conversation with the owner of that dog could potentially be spiritually fruitful. I invited the pastor to join me and headed straight for the group in the middle of the park. Although the conversation was pleasant, there was no spiritual interest that surfaced, so we turned to head back. After just a few steps, I suddenly felt a hand on my shoulder. The pastor and I turned and were greeted by a lady. She had spotted us from the other side of the park and had headed straight in our direction.

The lady was slightly inebriated, but was coherent. One of her first questions indicated that this would be a spiritual conversation and was no doubt a divine appointment, "Do you believe we came from star dust?"
A bit confused, I responded with a "No." "Do you believe in a higher power?" That was a question I could respond to in the affirmative. Meg had come to the park with her young adult daughter. Her husband was a doctor, as were both of her daughters. She was also in the medical field. Meg volunteered that she didn't like church because it seemed that all they wanted was money and power. She felt that churches should be more engaged in helping people who don't have advantages in life.

"It sounds like you wish the church would do the kind of things Jesus did when He was here on the earth?" That comment struck a chord with Meg.

"Yes, that is the type of church I would want to be a part of!" At this point, Meg shifted the conversation. "Maybe if my son had attended your school things would have turned out different for him." Meg shared that her son had been dating a young lady who had broken his heart. Not able to cope with the grief, at the age of twenty he had taken his own life. She now had a life mission to help other young people so that their story wouldn't end up like his. We were able to pray with her, and she gladly shared her contact information. The pastor and his wife were able to follow up with Meg. We were reminded how important it is to be aware of those around us. As we lift up our eyes (John 4:35), we will come in contact with many individuals like Meg who are looking for satisfying answers in their life.

Pray at the beginning of the day that God will give you a divine appointment; then journal the results here at the end of the day.

_____

_____

_____

_____

_____

_____

_____

_____

_____

_____

_____

_____

_____

_____

_____

Most employers believe that workers leave because they want to earn more money. This simply isn't true. "Only 12 percent of employees leave their company because of money. Instead, company culture is the primary culprit for turnover."[1]

Astute employers recognize the importance of building team.
People who enjoy being around each other will perform better and have increased loyalty. In order to accomplish this, team-building activities outside of the workplace are helpful. This gives relationships an opportunity to grow on a different level.[1]

As a visiting speaker at a meeting for ministers in Western Australia, I was excited and nervous when I was invited to play a game of paintball. There were two factors that made me nervous. First, we would be playing at night, and second, it was in the woods. The fear of encountering a snake was a much greater worry than the paint balls. As we divided into teams and headed out to take our respective positions, it was fascinating to see the relational dynamics. It was certainly different than sitting in a training session all day. When the executive secretary captured the flag from no man's land and ran it safely across the opposing team's side, the winners erupted in cheers. I haven't forgotten that experience and I'm sure the pastors have not either. A lasting bond was created that would have never occurred while just sitting in a room together.

The same principle applies when it comes to divine appointments. We may see someone every day at work or school. We may enjoy conversations and even have a friendship. Everything changes though when the context is shifted. Discover something they would enjoy doing together with you. It might be an activity like a game of golf, an excursion to an NBA game, dinner together, a hike in nature, a bike ride, a zoo trip, or a shared hobby. This is a great opportunity to include family members as well. It is amazing what the changed context does to the relationship. Give it a try!

---

[1] *"Ten Shocking Statistics About Disengaged Employees," Officevibe, April 3, 2017, https:// officevibe.com/blog/disengaged-employees-infographic.*

COACHING QUESTION

What current friendship would be taken to the next level by a change of context? What activity would they likely enjoy doing with you?

_____

_____

_____

_____

While completing graduate studies at Andrews University, I took a part-time job stocking grocery shelves at Meijer (a store similar to Walmart Supercenter). My typical shift was from ten o'clock in the evening to six-thirty in the morning. Needless to say, I occasionally nodded off during class the next day. One of the classes I took had a memorable assignment: make friends with an unchurched person by doing something with them outside of the context in which you currently know them. I knew plenty of unchurched people from my work. The only question was, which one should I befriend as a requirement for this class? I finally decided that Harry was the right person.

One challenge was that Harry headed to the smoking section when we were on break. Not to be deterred, I arranged to consistently stock shelves on the same aisle as Harry. As we got to know each other, I made a simple suggestion to him. I said, "Hey Harry, we should get together sometime outside of work." Harry made a recommendation that perhaps I might enjoy going to a club with him. I quickly jumped in with another option, and we ended up settling on going out to eat at a "greasy spoon" diner nearby our work. When I was introduced to Harry's wife, I couldn't believe it. Her name was Mary. As a theology student, I was familiar with a popular book that had just been published—*Inside the Mind of Unchurched Harry and Mary*.[2] Unbelievably, I had met a real Harry and Mary in Benton Harbor, Michigan.

The relationship with Harry blossomed from that point to a meal at my home, a visit to their home, and a trip to the hospital when their baby was sick. Harry truly became a friend. The encounter with unchurched Harry and Mary taught me something of critical importance—everyone needs a friend and will respond when we show ourselves friendly. Changing the context made the difference. This became much more than a class assignment; it became a way of life.

---

[2] *Lee Strobel, Inside the Mind of Unchurched Harry and Mary: How to Reach Friends and Family Who Avoid God and the Church (Grand Rapids, MI: Zondervan, 1993).*

Pray at the beginning of the day that God will give you a divine appointment; then journal the results here at the end of the day.

_____

_____

_____

_____

_____

_____

_____

_____

_____

_____

_____

_____

_____

_____

_____

_____

_____

_____

_____

_____

_____

Loneliness has been identified as the next big public health crisis. The United Kingdom has even appointed a minister of loneliness to help address the growing epidemic. A recent study concluded that three out of four Americans are lonely.[1]

In an article in the Harvard Business Review, the former surgeon general of the United States, Dr. Vivek H. Murthy, wrote: "Loneliness and weak social connections are associated with a reduction in lifespan similar to that caused by smoking 15 cigarettes a day and even greater than that associated with obesity."[2]

A biblical solution to loneliness is hospitality. Radical hospitality is opening your heart and home as a demonstration of the love of God. Hospitality is listed as a practice that all followers of Jesus should demonstrate in their lives (Romans 12:13). The literal translation of this verse is "pursuing a love of strangers." The key word here is "pursuing." Just as we are called to "pursue love" (1 Corinthians 14:1), hospitality is an area in which all Christians are encouraged to grow. There is a popular quote from an unknown author that states this idea well: "When you have more than you need, build a longer table, not a higher fence."

---

[1] *"High Prevalence and Adverse Health Effects of Loneliness in Community-Dwelling Adults across the Lifespan: Role of Wisdom as a Protective Factor," International Psychogeriatrics 31, no. 10 (December 2018): https://doi.org/10.1017/S1041610218002120.*

[2] *Vivek Murthy, "Work and the Loneliness Epidemic" The Harvard Business Review, September 27, 2017, https://hbr.org/cover-story/2017/09/work-and-the-loneliness-epidemic.*

When we are passionate about our faith, we want to share it. Hospitality is probably the most natural way to do that. A neighbor, co-worker, or person we have encountered through a divine appointment will be highly likely to accept an invitation to our home for a meal. We don't have to have a model home, be a gourmet cook, or have a sanguine personality. "There is a great work to be done, and if you go to your neighbor with your heart all warm and glowing with love, do you not think that you can find the key to unlock your neighbor's heart?"[3]

COACHING QUESTION

What is your next step to pursue hospitality? When will you take action?

_____

_____

_____

_____

_____

[3] Ellen Gould White, "Let Us Go Without the Camp," The Review and Herald, May 28, 1889, https://m.egwwritings.org/en/book/821.9684.

We were looking for a new-to-us van on a budget. Craigslist.org helped us pinpoint the solution to our vehicle search. We drove the one hour to the opposite side of the metroplex, to the suburb of Garland, and paid $4,100 for a van with a cracked windshield. I asked the seller if he knew anyone who fixed windshields. He immediately made a phone call and informed us that his friend could be at our house the next day to replace it. Sure enough, Margarito and his wife, Brenda, made the one-hour commute the following day.

As the windshield was being replaced, my wife and I visited with Margarito and Brenda. We learned how they had arrived in Texas and some of the foods they enjoyed. As the job was completed, my wife suggested that we should have them over sometime for Brazilian food. They responded readily to the idea, but no date was set (our first mistake). Margarito gave us a stack of business cards in case we had friends who ended up with broken windshields, and off they went. Unfortunately, we failed to make follow-up contact (our second mistake) and may have failed to ever see them again, except for providential circumstances.

It was time to replace our second vehicle with a new-to-us truck. Craigslist. org helped us again. This is where the unusual happened. I found a truck in the same suburb as the van, for the same price, and with the same problem—a broken windshield. I went straight to the kitchen drawer and found Margarito's card. I called to schedule an appointment to install the new windshield for our truck. This time, we scheduled a date for a meal in our home.

Margarito and Brenda brought their four children for lunch and soccer at our home. While the rest of the family went outside, Brenda stayed behind to help clean up and visit with my wife. Brenda shared some of the painful journey she had been through in recent years. A friendship was sparked. The family came back to visit again. Brenda and my wife spoke on the phone on a regular basis. We drove up closer to where they lived, and we all went to church together. When Brenda found out that our family was moving to Michigan, she asked my wife something remarkable: "Would you be willing for my daughter to come and live with you?" The circumstances did not allow for that to take place, but her request made a profound impact on us. The simple gesture of hospitality had opened their hearts.

PRAYER & JOURNAL CHALLENGE

Pray at the beginning of the day that God will give you a divine appointment; then journal the results here at the end of the day.

Soul winning is a collaboration between the Divine and humankind. There are aspects of the process that only God can do. Only God can fill us with the Holy Spirit. Only God can convert a human heart. Only God can perform miracles. In this equation, we also have a part to play. We are to testify of the difference God has made in our lives. We are to mingle and build relationships. We are to listen to the voice of the Holy Spirit and follow His instructions. Most importantly, we are to pray for God to direct our lives.

Proclamation evangelism (public evangelism) is the reaping stage of soul winning. Effectiveness in this phase requires proper soil preparation. Spiritual conversations and divine appointments are a starting point on the journey toward accepting Jesus. They are like drips in a bucket. Whenever someone makes a decision to be baptized, it is certain that drips have been added to their bucket over time and by many people, resulting in it overflowing.

Over the past thirty days, you have read of encounters that ultimately resulted in baptism. There are others that were simply a single drip (a drive-thru divine appointment) and some that were multiple drips (a dine-in divine appointment). What is our job? It is to add a drip or drips to the bucket. The ultimate decision to follow Jesus, the heart conversion, is something that only God can do.

I'd like to encourage you to continue the thirty-day challenge to day thirty, thirty-two, and for the rest of your life. The results will be life-changing, for both you and the people to whom God leads you.

COACHING QUESTION

What commitment will you make to pray for divine appointments on a daily basis?

_____

_____

_____

_____

A divine appointment is usually made up of two parties, those who need Jesus and those who are representing Him. More often than not, those involved don't usually have a full grasp of the weight of that particular situation, nor the circumstances that God had arranged to get the right people in the right place at the right time for Him to work miraculously. At least that was my experience when, as a seventeen-year-old, I met two female bible workers on my doorstep who asked me if I wanted to hang out with them. They had no idea that the conversation I was having with them would be so important, that I was in the perfect place to receive the gospel, and that the company they were offering was exactly what I needed.

Six months earlier I had returned to my home in Newcastle, Australia, after living for two years in Spain as an up-and-coming professional motorcycle racer. I had just finished a two-year stint in the junior world championship circuit, and out of nowhere my life just fell apart. My career went belly up, my parents split up and went bankrupt, and I just couldn't see a way forward. I went from an exceptional person to living with my dad, helping him every day to prepare our family house to be sold. In all of this, I just felt like a total failure

This whole situation led me to fall heavy into depression, alcoholism, self-harm, and eventually a suicide attempt. My parents, being worried, put me in a hospital on suicide watch where I spent six weeks being medicated and going through therapy. The day I was discharged, I moved into my sister's apartment. It was the next morning when the aforementioned bible workers knocked on my door.

Three years later, at the age of twenty-one, I am a baptized Seventh-day Adventist working full-time in ministry and evangelism, as well as radio host on FaithFM. My life has completely changed by the grace of God, and that is all because two young women asked me to hang out with them when I was seventeen years old.

Pray at the beginning of the day that God will give you a divine appointment; then journal the results here at the end of the day.

_____

_____

_____

_____

_____

_____

_____

_____

_____

_____

_____

_____

_____

_____

_____

_____

_____

_____